Minibeasts are little animals all around you. They live in the garden, in your home and even on you!

Many minibeasts creep or crawl across the ground. Others have amazing bodies that fly or swim. Watch out, some of them sting!

Minibeast

Wasp

Most minibeasts are
very small.

Some of them could sit on
your finger, like this moth.
Others could fit in your hand.

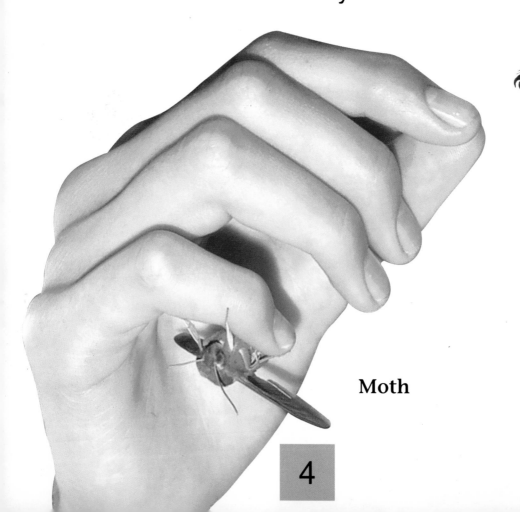

Moth

4

REALLY ABOUT

Minibeasts

by Janet Allison Brown

Aladdin/Watts
London • Sydney

Contents

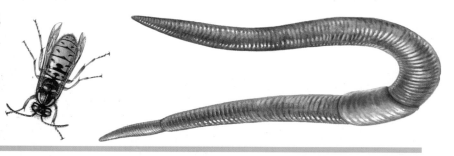

© Aladdin Books Ltd 2000

Designed and produced by
Aladdin Books Ltd
28 Percy Street
London W1T 2BZ

First published in
Great Britain in 2000 by
Franklin Watts
96 Leonard Street
London EC2A 4XD

ISBN 0 7496 4848 1

A catalogue record for this book is
available from the British Library.

Printed in the U.A.E.

All rights reserved

Editor
Jim Pipe

Literacy Consultant
Phil Whitehead
Oxford Brookes University
Westminster Institute of Education

Design
Flick, Book Design and Graphics

Picture Research
Brian Hunter Smart

Snail

Ants

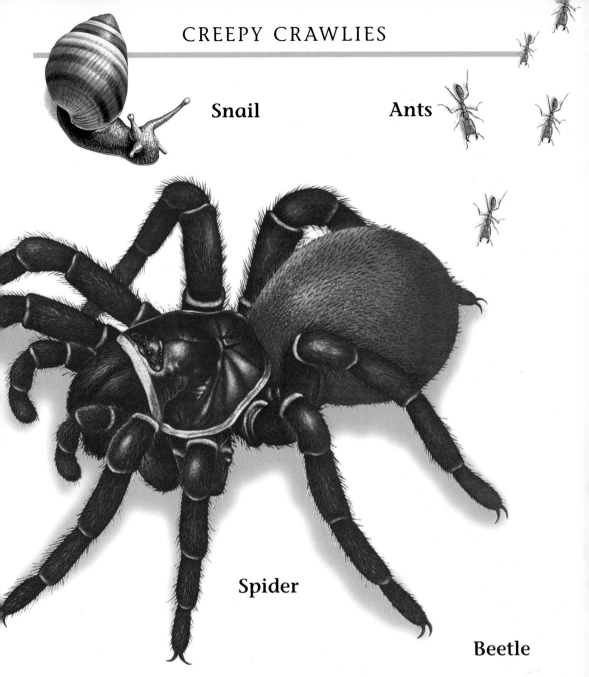

Spider

Beetle

Would you like this
beetle to land on you?

Most minibeasts have tiny legs. This ladybird can crawl or fly.

Cockroaches creep around at night, looking for food. If you are quiet, you may hear them crawl.

Cockroaches

Ladybird

Where are its wings?

Close up, spiders can look scary. See this tarantula creep up the wall on its long legs. It grabs other animals with its big jaws.

Its body looks soft and hairy. Would you like to touch it?

Jaws

Tarantula
Spiders have
eight legs.

9

Slugs and snails have just one big, slimy foot. They move very, very slowly.

Snails have a shell on their back. This is their home and they carry it around with them.

Slug

Snail

Like snails, worms do not have legs. They move by wriggling their long, pink bodies in the earth.

Earthworm

Beetles also have a shell on their back. It is hard like armour. It covers their body and wings.

Many beetles smell with their long feelers. Other minibeasts taste with their feet! Can you do that?

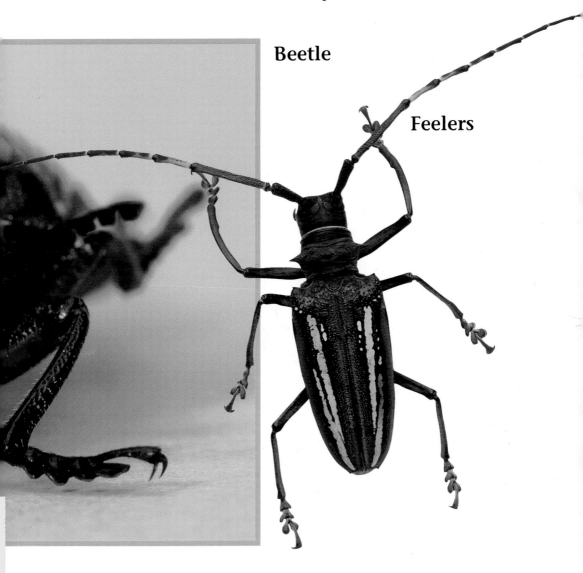

Beetle

Feelers

13

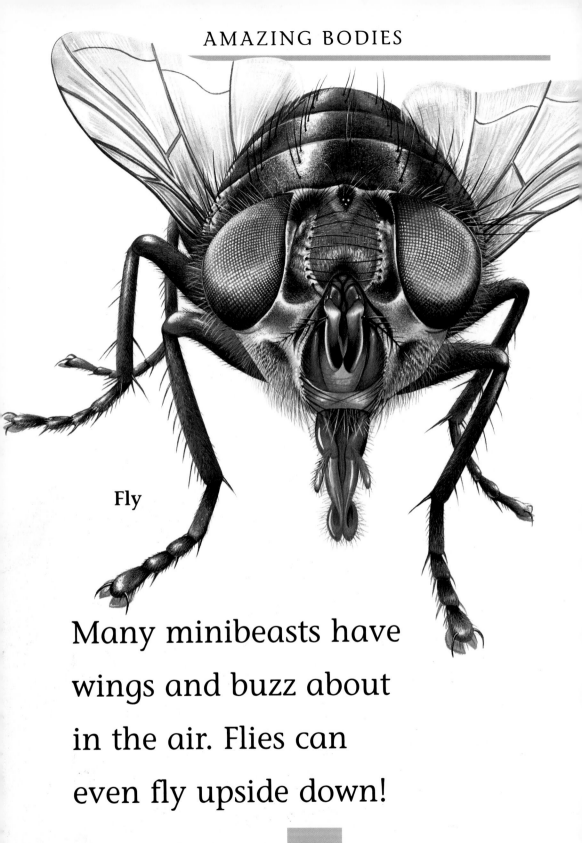

Fly

Many minibeasts have
wings and buzz about
in the air. Flies can
even fly upside down!

A fly's big eyes are good at
spotting things that move.
So they are very hard to catch.

Maggots look like worms – but
they are really baby flies!

Maggots

Some minibeasts lay traps to catch food. Spiders spin sticky nets called webs.

When flies and bugs fly into the web, they get stuck. Then the spider crawls over the web to eat its dinner!

Spinning a web

1   2   3

Web spider

What shape is a web?

Moth

Can you see its feelers?

Birds and other animals eat minibeasts like this moth. So the moth only flies about at night.

It looks like a flower so it can hide during the day. Would you try to pick it?

Stick insect

Many minibeasts look like plants so they can hide.

Can you see the stick insect hiding in the picture above?

20

This hairy caterpillar is bright red, to tell birds that it tastes nasty.

A caterpillar chews leaves with its big jaws. But a fly has a mouth that sucks up food like a straw.

Caterpillar

The bombardier beetle squirts poison at animals that attack it.

Squirt!

Stink bugs let off a bad smell. This tells mice and other animals to keep away.

Stink bugs

Scorpion

Other minibeasts use stings to stop attackers, and to catch animals they want to eat.

A scorpion's sting is very painful, even for a big animal like you.

Nest

Like scorpions, wasps have a
nasty sting in their tail.
They live in nests made of
mud or of paper.

Some nests are very big, and lots of wasps live in them.

Wasps sometimes buzz around in gangs called swarms. If you see one, keep out of the way!

Wasps

Millions of ants live in this nest. Each ant has a job. The queen lays eggs. Workers look for food and soldier ants defend the nest.

Would you like them to run around in your house?

Ant nest
Look how many
ants there are!

Can You Find?

Minibeasts have strange and wonderful bodies. Can you tell which minibeast these body parts come from?

Wings

Jaws

Shell

Sting

Answers
on page 32.

Eyes

Feelers

Clue: Look at pages 8,
10, 13, 14, 18 and 24.

Do You Know?

Minibeasts can be found all over the place! Do you know where these minibeasts live?

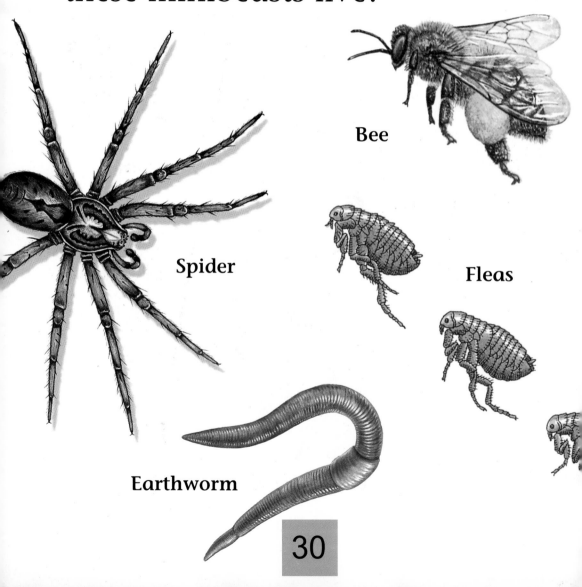

Bee

Spider

Fleas

Earthworm

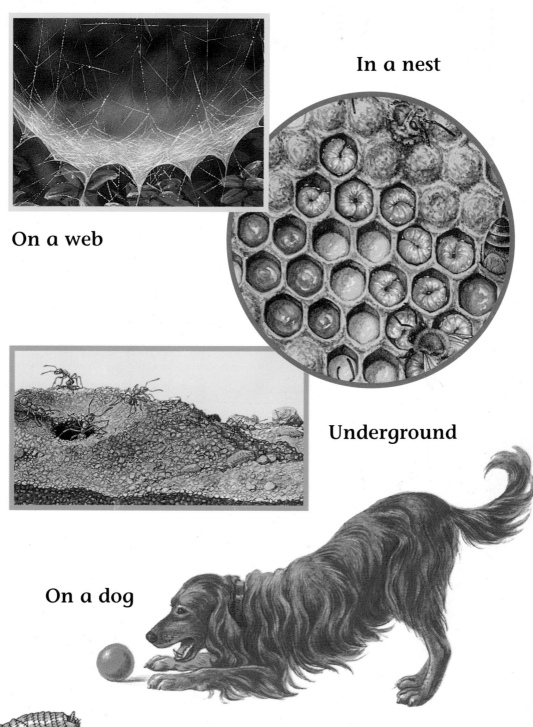

On a web

In a nest

Underground

On a dog

The answers are on page 32.

Index

ANSWERS TO QUESTIONS

Pages 28-29 – A spider has these **jaws** • A snail has this **shell** • A moth has these **wings** • A wasp has this **sting** • A fly has these **eyes** • A beetle has these **feelers**.

Pages 30-31 – A **bee** lives **in a nest** • **Fleas** live **on a dog** • An **earthworm** lives **underground** • A **spider** lives **on a web**.

Photocredits: Abbreviations: t-top, m-middle, b-bottom, r-right, l-left.
Cover, 7 – Ralph A Clevenger/CORBIS. 1, 3, 8-9, 12 – Stockbyte. 4, 6, 11, 18-19, 20, 28r – Select Pictures. 10, 28b – John Foxx Images.
16-17 – Corbis. 21 – Michael & Patricia Fogden/BBC Natural History Unit. 23 – Peter Oxford/BBC Natural History Unit.
25 – Borrell Casals/FLPA-Images of Nature. 26-27 – Andrew Cooper/BBC Natural History Unit.
Illustrators: David Cook, Tony Swift, Myke Taylor; Simon Turvey – Wildlife Art Ltd; Philip Weare, Norman Weaver.